The role of the Disability Practitioner within Post-16 education

National Association of Disability Practitioners (NADP) Briefing

Dr James M Palfreman-Kay

Contents

1. Executive Summary

This National Association of Disability Practitioners [NADP] Briefing aims to provide an update on *"Disability Officers in Higher Education",* which was written by Eileen Laycock[1] and published in 2001.

An electronic survey was sent out to practitioners between March and June 2007 through a number of JISCmail electronic discussion lists. Paper copies of the survey were also sent out to any individuals who requested a copy or who were not members of the NADP email lists. Therefore the data reported here represents a "snapshot" of the respondents between March and June 2007.

The survey was divided into three sections, which asked the respondents questions about NADP, themselves (the practitioners) and their role.

This NADP briefing on the role of a disability practitioner obtained a total of 112 responses and 63 of these (and one pending) reported that they were NADP members (at the time the NADP had 599 members). The survey reveals a varied picture of staff working within the post-16 sector to support disabled students. The results show that the majority of the respondents are members of NADP. In most cases people held Institutional or full membership of NADP.

The findings suggest that the terms Manager, Coordinator, Adviser, Assessor and Tutor are titles typically used to describe the work of staff within the sector. The institutional location of posts is usually within a Student Services department. Most practitioners reported that they are employed on a full-time basis on either an academic or administrative (professional & support staff) contract.

Respondents said that they brought a range of experience to the role, typically experience of working with disabled students in post-16 education or undertaking legislative and strategic work.

In delivering support to students, most of the respondents reported that they had been working within the sector either between 0-3 or 9-12 years. Most people said that for their role a bachelor's degree is the essential requirement, some posts required postgraduate or specialist qualifications. Some of the posts required respondents to have a range of specialist qualities, knowledge or skills.

In undertaking their day-to-day work, practitioners report there are 27 areas of activity. The priority activities include keeping up-to-date with disability legislation, supporting students, working with institutional staff or helping students to access relevant sources of funding. Other areas of activity may include responsibility for managing services or budgets, working with placement providers or undertaking outreach work.

---

[1] Formerly McCabe

2. Introduction

The aim of this report is to update the first NADP[2] briefing which was entitled *"Disability Officers in Higher Education"*[3] which was published in 2001. The aim of that publication was to investigate "disability officers, their work roles and information needs." (2001, page 2). During the 2005-2006 academic year a decision was taken by the NADP board to update this publication to reflect the changes within the sector and to provide an update on the role of disability practitioners working within the post-16 sector. The difference between the current briefing and the earlier publication is that the former investigates the role of disability practitioners working within Further and Higher Education.

For the purpose of this survey the term *"disability practitioner"* is used for any individual who is working to support disabled students studying with post-16 education.

In order to collect the views of disability practitioners working within the sector, an electronic survey was designed to provide the data for the updated briefing. An electronic survey was selected in preference to other methods of data collection, as it was believed an electronic survey would be a quick and effective way of reaching practitioners working within the post-16 sector.

The questions for the survey were based on three sources. These were compiled from suggestions by delegates at the annual NADP 2006 conference[4], feedback from Executive Board members and a review of the questions asked in the 2001 survey.

To launch the survey an email was sent to a selected number of JISCmail discussion lists[4] during the summer of 2007. A small number of questionnaires were also sent directly to some NADP members who are not members of the NADP email lists.

A total of 112 respondents completed the questionnaire.[5] These individuals provided quantitative and qualitative responses to the 25 questions. Those responses have been collated and analysed and are reported in section 4 of this report. Appendices 1-4 detail (1) the JISCmail discussion lists which were contacted to support the work, (2) the survey and all the (3) qualitative and (4) quantitative responses.

---

[2] Information about NADP can be found at http://www.nadp.org.uk

[3] This publication can be found electronically on the NADP members section of its website at the following url:
http://www.nadpuk.org/members/index.php?page=resources/publications

[4] Delegates attending *"The Future Direction of NADP – an insight into where NADP has come from and where the organisation will go in the future"* workshop. NADP Annual Conference and Annual General Meeting. Holiday Inn Birmingham, 2006. Individuals who attended this workshop were asked to comment on the proposed survey questions. Feedback from this workshop resulted in the proposed survey being amended.

[4] Appendix 1 lists the selected email lists.

[5] 5 responses were disregarded as they were duplicates.

3. Questionnaire Results

A total of 112 respondents working within post-16 education answered the 25 questions. The results have been organised under 3 headings. These are responses to:

- NADP questions
- practitioner questions
- job role questions.

3.1 NADP questions

The first part of the survey asked the respondents questions related to NADP. These included whether or not the respondents were members of the organisation as well as the length and type of membership held.

3.1.1 NADP membership

At the time of sending out the survey there were 599 members of NADP.[6] 63 members (plus one person whose membership was pending) responded. Whilst this response rate (63/599 = 10.52%) is relatively small, response rates of 10% - 25% are considered typical for unsolicited questionnaires.

The responses from members and non-members help provide an insight into the work of practitioners who are supporting disabled students within the post-16 sector.

Table 1: Response to briefing questionnaire

Yes/No	Frequency
Yes	63
No	47
Pending	1

The overall figure of 112 responses is higher than the 2001 survey, which drew 74 responses[7]. Given the substantial increase in the number of disabled students over the last ten years, one might expect that the number of practitioners working in the sector to support disabled students would have increased since 2001, though there are no official statistics on this.

---

[6] This figure was based on the April 2007 Board membership report.

[7] In the 2001 survey 13 responses were rejected as unusable because they were either not completed by Disability Officers or had not been completed correctly.

3.1.2 Length of NADP membership

The responses[8] summarised in Table 2 show that the majority of the members who completed the survey had held NADP membership for up to 3 years. Only 11 respondents had been members of NADP for at least 6 years.

Table 2: Respondents' duration of NADP membership

Number of Years of membership of NADP	Frequency
Under 1 year	9
1	6
2	12
3	7
4	8
5	8
6	10
6+ years	1
Other	1

It is pleasing to see that so many less experienced practitioners join NADP as we aim to provide a source of professional support and development for people who are new to the sector.

It is also important to note the participation of long standing members, whose contribution often helps to support the development of the less experienced practitioners e.g. through conferences etc.

---

[8] There were 8 qualitative responses in total to this question (3), which can be found at Appendix 3 on page 48.

3.1.3 Category of membership

Table 3 shows that the majority of the respondents held institutional or full membership of NADP.[9]

Table 3: NADP membership categories

Category of membership	Frequency
Institutional	32
Additional Institutional	2
Full	19
Associate	7
Student	0
Retired	0
International	0
Affiliate	0
Not answered	1

3.2 Responses to practitioner questions

The second part of the survey asked the respondents questions about themselves. These were their gender; whether or not they had an impairment; whether or not they had disclosed this to their employer.

3.2.1 Gender

Table 4: Respondents' gender

Gender	Frequency
Male	18
Female	88
Not answered	1

Table 4 shows that the majority of respondents who completed the survey were female. The high response rate from women may suggest that disability support within post-16 education is mainly undertaken by women.

---

[9] Information about the types of membership available to practitioners wishing to join NADP can be found at: http://www.nadp-uk.org/membership/

3.2.2 Disability

The qualitative responses[10] suggest the majority of respondents who are working within the post-16 sector do not consider themselves to have a direct personal experience of impairment.

Table 5: Respondents and disability

Personal experience of impairment	Frequency
Yes	25
No	75
No response	12

The individuals who identified themselves as having impairments disclosed a range of impairments e.g. dyslexia, visual impairment and being registered blind. One respondent indicated that they would not normally disclose their impairment in this survey, but would identify themselves as being a disabled person.

3.2.3 Disclosure of disability

When comparing the responses to question 6 with question 5, the majority of disabled practitioners had disclosed to their employer. The support provided to staff is funded through the Access to Work programme.

Table 6: Disclosure of disability to their employer

Disclosure	Frequency
Yes	20
No	3
No reply	2

A review of the qualitative responses[11] suggests that staff may not be receiving support for a number of reasons. These are finding little proactive support from their employer and often having to arrange the assistance themselves.

A summary of these negative experiences, as evidenced in the qualitative responses, is listed below.

---

[10] There were 6 qualitative responses in total to this question (5), which can be found at Appendix 3 on page 48.

[11] There were 9 qualitative responses in total to this question (6), which can be found at Appendix 3 on pages 48-49.

"It is extremely difficult to be positive about my employer's attitude towards staff with disabilities. I will not even go into what they do to students. It is all lip-service. No, no substance!" (HE Respondent)

"Although I disclosed in 2004, little has been done to support me, in spite of an Access to Work assessment and recommendations being sent to HR."
(HE Respondent)

"Yes, I have disclosed but no, I do not think appropriate support is being provided."
(FE Respondent)

The responses suggest that when practitioners disclose their own impairment and seek support, they will receive some assistance. However, the extent and quality of that assistance seems to vary across institutions.

3.3 Job role questions

The third part of the survey asked the respondents questions related to their job role. These included job title, employment status and numbers of students.

3.3.1 Job Title

There were seventy-four different job titles[12] provided by the respondents who completed the survey.

Table 7: Practitioner job titles

Job title	Frequency
Disability Adviser	12
Disability Co-ordinator	7
Disability Services Manager	3
DSA Assessor	3
Dyslexia Co-ordinator	2
Dyslexia Support Tutor	2
Senior Disability Adviser	3

The job titles "Disability Adviser" and "Disability Co-ordinator" were the two most reported terms. Disability Services Manager, DSA Assessor and Senior Disability Adviser were the next most commonly used job titles.

The terminology **Manager, Co-ordinator, Adviser, Assessor** and **Tutor** suggest that practitioners are, broadly-speaking, undertaking 5 areas of activity when working with disabled students.

---

[12] See Appendix 3 pages 49-50 for a listing of all the job titles provided by each respondent.

3.3.2 Employment

The majority of the respondents who completed the survey were employed on a full-time contract, with a smaller number on part-time contracts and an even smaller number self-employed or hourly paid.

Table 8: Employment status

Category	Frequency
Full-time contract	85
Part-time contract	19
Self-employed	2
Hourly paid	1
Other	1

One of the qualitative responses[13] suggests how these contracts might work in practice.

"I am employed directly by the university on a contract basis of 400 hours per year and also take on extra DSA referrals which are LEA funded."
(HE Respondent).

The responses suggest that job contracts are sometimes funded from external funding streams such as the Disabled Students' Allowance (DSA).

3.3.3 Employer

The majority of the respondents were working within HE when they completed the survey, with the second highest response coming from individuals working within FE. In total 83 respondents[14] disclosed the type of institution they worked for, whether that was for a:

- University
- College of Further Education
- Sixth Form College
- Public / Private Assessment Centre
- Local Education Authority
- National Charity

For Higher Education, 53 respondents disclosed their employer and these have been sorted into recognised groups or listings[15] which are represented in Table 9b.

---

[13] There were 3 qualitative responses in total to this question (8), which can be found at Appendix 3 on page 51.

[14] To maintain the privacy of the respondents who disclosed for whom they worked, the responses to this question have been sorted into recognised sector groups or geographical areas. The numbers within either the sector group or region represent the total number of institutions.

[15] The source for this data has been taken from the for Higher Education Research Opportunities [HERO] website: http://www.hero.ac.uk/uk/home/index.cfm

For Further Education, 24 respondents disclosed their employer and these have been sorted into recognised regions identified by the Association of Colleges for England, Wales and Scotland[16]. The colleges are categorised by region in table 9c.

Table 9a: Respondents employer broken by organisation

Organisation	Frequency
FE College	26
Specialist College	1
University	74
Public Assessment Centre	3
Private Assessment Centre	1
IT Supplier	0
Other	5

Table 9b: HE employer broken down by sector group or listing

Employer's Group / listing	Frequency
Russell Group (20)	13
1994 Group (19)	4
Guild HE (29)	4
University Alliance (22)	11
Pre-1992 (43)	9
Million+ (31)	12

Table 9c: FE respondents broken down region

Regions	Number
East Midlands (24)	1
Eastern Region (33)	3
Greater London (55)	1
North Western (51)	1
Northern Ireland (6)	1
Scotland (43)	1
Northern Region (21)	3
South Eastern (60)	6
South Western (30)	3
Wales (25)	0
West Midlands (45)	0
Yorkshire and Humberside (36)	1

---

[16] The source for this data has been taken from the Association of Colleges website for England and Wales website:
http://www.aoc.co.uk/en/

The qualitative responses[17] to this question outlined the range of employers for whom the respondents worked.

"I also do 2 days per week on a temporary hourly paid contact at XXX University as an XXX Adviser." (HE & Private Sector Assessment Centre Respondent)

"It's an NNAC/QAG-listed centre in an FE College." (FE Respondent)

"This is a small (250 students) specialist contemporary dance college with a Foundation Course, Bachelor of Performing Arts course and Graduate courses." (FE Respondent)

The data in Table 9a suggests most respondents were employed by either Russell Group, Million+ or the University Alliance. For FE, the majority of respondents came from the South Eastern region. The range of employers the respondents work for shows that disabled students are studying at a range of institutions, which requires an appropriate level of support to be in place.

3.3.4 Providing support to disabled students

The respondents reported having worked supporting disabled students for periods identified in Table 10.

Table 10: Length of experience in supporting disabled students

Years	Frequency of Staff responses
0-3	15
3-6	27
6-9	22
9-12	18
Other	15

The qualitative responses[18] confirm that staff are supporting disabled students through a number of roles. For example:

"I provide support for disabled students in the School of XXX and XXX and advise colleagues on disability issues. I liaise with the Disability Officer on behalf of students and staff in our School." (HE Respondent)

"I have taught in post-16 [education] for 24 years of which 10 [years] has been as an assessor and support tutor and undertaking staff development. Prior to that my work as a tutor has an inclusive education profile." (HE Respondent)

---

[17] There were 7 qualitative responses in total to this question (10), which can be found in Appendix 3 on page 51.

[18] There were 23 qualitative responses to this question (11), which can be found in Appendix 3 on pages 51-53.

"My current role involves supporting disabled staff, but sometimes this includes people who are both a member of staff and a student (e.g. Graduate Teaching Assistant / PhD student)." (HE Respondent)

"14 years including previous HEFCE-funded project in XXX University."
(HE Respondent)

"Myself currently 13 years, but the University for 15 years as having a named adviser."
(HE Respondent)

The responses show the roles undertaken range from acting as a central point of contact for a school or institution to undertaking project work or specific disability roles. The variation suggests that each institution has developed in its own approach to supporting disabled students, probably as a result of institutional need.

3.3.5 Length of service

The responses in Table 11 show that the majority of the respondents have been working in their current post between 0 and 8 years. The majority of responses came from individuals who have been working in their current role between 2 and 5 years.

Table 11: Time in current post

Time in current post (years)	Number of respondents
0-2	28
2-5	38
5-8	25
8-11	8
11-14	6
Other	3

The respondents' experience of supporting disabled students in their current role was varied.[19]

"My post is academic and the disability part is additional to my academic duties. It was not considered in the recent pay framework job evaluation."
(HE Respondent)

"In the early part of my time here I also taught groups of adults with learning disabilities at Entry and Level 1 - Life Skills, Literacy, Numeracy, Independent living skills."
(FE Respondent)

---

[19] There were 4 qualitative responses in total to this question (12) which can be found in Appendix 3 on page 53.

These responses show that one respondent had a disability role added to their academic duties, whilst another had become involved in supporting this group of learners through a teaching route.

3.3.6 Location of posts within organisation

As one might anticipate, the majority of the posts, as outlined in Table 12, are located within Student Services.

Table 12: Location of disability post

Location	Frequency
Student Services	70
Registry	3
Academic Services	15
Other	20
Study Support	1

Whilst Table 12 shows Student Services is the main location for disability posts, the qualitative responses[20] shows practitioners have mixed views about whether or not this is an appropriate location.

"School of XXX. For some bizarre reason we were located within one academic school, and taken away from Student Support."
(FE Respondent)

"Locating the service in academia is vital to ensure change to practice is more effective – role includes exam boards and validations. etc.." (HE Respondent)

"I am not convinced that Student Services is the correct place for support for disabled students." (HE Respondent)

These responses show that at least two respondents feel the support for disabled students should be located within an academic setting, whilst another feels it should be moved from an academic setting and re-located within Student Support.

Whilst Table 12 identifies a number of locations for disability posts within an institution or company, the respondents highlighted a number of other places. These are:

- Academic School
- Equality Service or Unit
- Skills for Life
- Business Support
- Library Services
- Occupational Health
- Skills for Life-Study Support

---

[20] There were 26 qualitative responses in total to this question (13), which can be found in Appendix 3 on pages 53-54.

- Learner Services
- Research Laboratory

The other institutional locations of disability posts show that support for disabled students is being provided in a number of areas, whether that is through the delivery of specific services or research based work. It is noted that the range of different locations mainly come from staff working within Further Education.

3.3.7 Qualifications

The responses recorded in Table 13 suggest that a bachelor's degree is the main qualification required for undertaking a disability-related role within the post-16 sector. Post-graduate and specialist qualifications are held by a number of respondents.

Table 13: Qualifications held by respondents

Qualification	Frequency
Degree	56
Postgraduate degree	19
Management	4
Specialist	17
Other	9

Examples of the range of postgraduate and specialist qualifications held by the respondents are:

- Interpreting and British Sign Language (BSL) qualifications
- OCR Certificate in Specific Learning Difficulties (SpLD)
- Specialist dyslexia qualification (e.g. AMBDA)
- Masters Degree in Special Educational Needs
- Teaching qualification

Some respondents reported that they had, or were being supported to obtain, management qualifications based on experience in their current role. Whilst the majority of the respondents showed they had required some form of recognised qualification to obtain their role, the qualitative responses[21] also revealed that knowledge and experience was identified as an important part of the role.

"Experience, but also had a nursing background. The job has been evolving rapidly and my previous experience has been invaluable to help me to manage staff and develop this role. There has been little on training for disability across the college for teaching staff, so I have had to find my way independently." (FE Respondent)

"Experience. I trained as a Needs Assessor at XXX, after completing a B.Sc. (Hons.) in Business Information Systems at XXX University."
(HE Respondent)

---

[21] There were 33 qualitative responses in total to this question (14), which can be found in Appendix 3 on pages 54-56.

"While no specific formal qualifications were required for the post. It did ask that candidates have knowledge and experience of working with students with disabilities." (FE Respondent)

"There were no qualification requirements. Previous experience, aptitude and being a friend of someone already doing the job were the key factors." (FE Respondent)

"Knowledge and experience of sector required." (HE Respondent)

These responses suggest that, for at least some disability posts, there is more of an emphasis being placed on knowledge and experience, rather than a recognised qualification.

3.3.8 Previous experience

The respondents[22] had brought a range of experience to their posts. Their experiences have been organised under three headings:

- Public sector or post-16 education
- Disabled students and post-16 education
- Policy, legislation and funding

Some of the respondents had not worked in disability be5#fore, but described other experience or having worked within the public sector or other roles within the post-16 education.

"Working in University for a long time but no experience in disability save for experience as parent of disabled child." (HE Respondent)

"Previous role involved co-ordinating exam / academic support for students with additional needs, otherwise I didn't have any direct disability-related experience." (HE Respondent)

"Extensive experience of working in the public sector including the Civil Service and the NHS. Also worked for a large customer service department for a major industrial company." (HE Respondent)

Others had extensive experience working with disabled students within the post-16 sector through acting as a manager of a number of services.

"Experience of working with disabled students for over 15 years. Experience of assessing for DSA – previous ACCESS Centre Manager." (HE Respondent)

"Working with students since 1988, providing ALL student services. Specialised in "disability" support since 1991." (HE Respondent)

---

[22] There were 96 qualitative responses in total to this question (15), which can be found in Appendix 3 on pages 56-63.

"I worked in FE as a lecturer to students with learning difficulties and/or physical disabilities, Mental health Co-ordinator and finally ALS Manager, managing 50 support staff and a budget of [more than a million pounds]*."*
(HE & Private Sector Assessment Centre Respondent)

Some of the respondents came from a specialism which involved disability work such as a residential setting or providing 1:1 support for students.

"2 years support work with people with disabilities-residential / community.
1 year support work with people with learning difficulties-employment."
(HE Respondent)

"Substantial experience in D/deaf education, all sectors inc HE, BSL/English interpreter, MA in Deaf Studies, knowledge of DSA Assessments, as a trainer inc of staff to work with D/deaf & disabled students." (HE Respondent)

"I had 10 years experience working with students with dyslexia and study skills problems."
(FE Respondent)

"Three years f/t needs assessing, with experience in Visual Impairment, Hearing Impairment, and Mobility Issues." (HE Respondent)

Other respondents came from a background of working on policy, legislation or funding:

"Over 20 years experience in CRE as policy officer, then senior policy officer. 2 years experience of equality and diversity work in another university."
(HE Respondent)

"Experience in interpreting the DDA and providing support to colleagues as well as influencing senior stakeholders. No previous experience in the education sector."
(HE Respondent)

"Previous work in higher education institution and also background in Disability funding."
(HE Respondent)

The responses suggest that the respondents are being required to demonstrate a range of experiences within their current roles, whether that is experience of managing or co-ordinating services, providing specific support or advice on policy, legislation or funding.

3.3.9 Specialist qualities, knowledge or skills

The responses to this question[23] suggest that some individuals were required to have specialist qualities, knowledge or skills to undertake their role, whereas other did not. To reflect this difference, the responses have been organised under two headings, which are:

- Requirement for specialist qualities, knowledge and skills
- No specialist qualities, knowledge and skills required

---

[23] There were 84 qualitative responses in total to this question (16), which can be found in Appendix 3 on pages 64-68.

Examples of specialist qualities, knowledge and skills required to undertake their current role include knowledge of assistive software to knowledge of specific disabilities, of management and or of legislation.

"Braille, Music Reading, Music Computer skills, Disability Awareness Training experience, Assistive software." (HE Respondent)

"I think both roles require an in-depth knowledge of the support requirements of students with learning difference, physical and hidden disabilities. An understanding of the human condition helps and also having knowledge of how to set boundaries and a sense of empathy aids the process of organising appropriate support. Utilising open questions and active listening is vital and knowledge of the institution's systems is important!"
(HE & Private Sector Assessment Centre Respondent)

"Verbal and written communication skills / listening & interviewing skills, including the ability to respond with sensitivity and empathy to students in distress / Analytical thinking & creative problem-solving skills / ability to develop & deliver training courses Knowledge of assistive technology and ICT skills / An understanding of general disability issues as they affect higher education / An understanding of a wide range of specific physical and mental impairments and the ability to translate this into practical support strategies for students in higher education." (HE Respondent)

"Team management and experience, knowledge and experience of working with disabled people. Knowledge of DDA and DED presentation, communication skills etc."
(FE Respondent)

"Full Teaching qualification, specialist Post Grad. (I hold a Post Grad cert in Aspergers) management experience and training." (FE Respondent)

Other respondents reported that they were not required to have specialist qualities, knowledge or skills to undertake their role.   The responses suggest generic skills are important. Examples given ranged from "good people and organisational skills" to "knowledge and experience of higher education".

"No, but it has hugely benefited from my experience." (FE Respondent)

"Not particularly but good organisational and people skills help."
(FE Respondent)

"Not particularly but good organisational and people skills help."
(HE Respondent)

"General experience and understanding of HE." (HE Respondent)

Generally, the responses suggest that, whilst it is important to have specialist qualities, knowledge and skills to undertake some roles, employers do not always consider these an essential requirement to work within a post-16 disability environment.

3.3.10 Contract and grade

The responses suggest respondents are, as one might expect, typically employed either on academic[24] or administrative /support contracts.[25] Some of the respondents reported that they were being moved across to the National Pay Framework, which is based upon a single pay spine.[26] The majority of practitioners reported that they were being placed on the nationally agreed pay spine instead of a local variation.

Table 14: Contracts of Employment

Contract	Frequency
Academic	43
Academic-related	0
Administrative and support	31
Local variation to the National Pay Framework	1
National Pay Framework	10
Self-employed	2
Permanent	19
Temporary	3
Fractional	0
Term-Time Only	1
Other	4

The qualitative[27] responses also indicate that practitioners are employed on a number of different contracts.

"An AR grade would be much more appropriate as the majority of my tasks are not administrative." (HE Respondent)

"I had an academic contract as a dyslexia tutor in another HEI, but local contract in the current HEI." (HE Respondent)

---

[24] The grades on which staff were employed were 2,3,4,6,7,8. Other academic grades listed were: Manager grade D (teachers scale); HERA 7; Lecture B and Senior Lecture.

[25] The grades on which staff were employed on were 4,5,6,7,8. Other administrative and support grades listed were: PO3:MG9F;POD/E;PO1;SEO;SE02.

[26] One respondent was employed on a local variation to the National Pay Framework spine point (Grade 8). 10 respondents were employed on the National Pay Framework (e.g. 5,6,7,8). Examples of these grades were: 6,7,7,8,7,5 and FE band D, 7, 28.

[27] There were 15 qualitative responses in total to this question (17), which can be found in Appendix 3 on page 69.

"Permanent post. Just transferred to national single pay spine." (HE Respondent)

"Just moved onto new pay scale so cannot give current grade. Now called professional and support." (HE Respondent)

Whilst the responses show that the respondents were employed on different contracts, it is also evident that some of the individuals felt the role should be viewed as an academic instead of an administrative role.

3.3.11 Salary

The majority of the responses for a disability practitioner ranged between £25,000 and £35,000 per year. The next most common salary bands were £15,000 - £25,000 and £35,000 - £45,000.

Table 15: Respondents' salaries

Salary	Frequency[28]
under £15,000	3
£15,000-£25,000	18
£25,000-£35,000	66
£35,000-£45,000	18
£45,000 upwards	2

The qualitative responses[29] suggest that some staff felt the work they were undertaking was not being sufficiently recognised by their current salary.

"We are underpaid and undervalued." (HE Respondent)

"It is less than an equivalent post at most of the other universities." (HE Respondent)

"At the bottom end of this scale. I think HERA has made a wider gap between pay of colleagues in high level support roles (such as disability adviser) in different universities. Everything is more variable now not standardised at all as was promised."
(HE Respondent)

The responses suggest that some respondents feel there is a variation of salaries for equivalent roles between institutions, which may be creating a feeling of resentment for some individuals.

---

[28] These figures include part-time and term-time only posts.

[29] There were 6 qualitative responses in total to this question (18), which can be found in Appendix 3 page 70.

3.3.12 Funding of post

Funding for the majority of the respondents' posts is from central institutional funds. The next most common source of funding was a combination of funding streams, as identified below, which could be Disabled Students' Allowance, Disability Premium or Learning and Skills Council funding.

The qualitative responses[30] also support the conclusion that practitioner posts are funded from a number of sources. Examples of the funding sources mentioned are:

- Disability premium and DSA funding
- DSA; LSC; ALS funding; Work Based Training funding
- Project funding, e.g. LSC, ESF, Lottery, grants, etc.

Table 16: Funding for disability practitioner posts

Funding source	Frequency
Disability premium funding	9
Institutional funds	33
Disabled Students' Allowance funding	8
Access to Learning Funding	0
Learning and Skills Council funding	15
A combination of the above	23
Don't Know	12
Other	7

One respondent reported that the service they worked for was expected to be mainly self-funded.

"All activities in the centre are income generating – no direct funding. So mainly via the DSA." (HE Respondent)

As one might anticipate, the funding of disability support within the post-16 sector is drawn from a number of funding sources available to the organisation for which an individual is working.

3.3.13 Numbers of disabled students

55 institutions contributed responses, which are summarised in Table 17. The data shows that most institutions had between 100 and 1000 disabled students and these represent between 1-20% of the institution's students.

A small number of institutions had either very high or very low numbers of disabled students: 7 institutions had less than 100 disabled students, but these represent between 5 and100% of the student body (the latter presumably a small institution specialising in

---

[30] There were 18 qualitative responses in total to this question (19), which can be found in Appendix 3 pages 70-71.

disabled students). Three institutions had more than 2500 disabled students but these were obviously very large universities as the disabled cohort represented only 6-7% of all students.

Table 17: Numbers of disabled students

Number of Institutions	Number of disabled students	Percentage of the Institution's students who disclose an impairment
7	0-100	5% – 100%[31]
25	100-500	4% - 20%
30	500-1000	1% - 10%
14	1000-1500	6% - 12%
11	1500-2000	3.8% – 10%
2	2000-2500	9% - 10%
3	2500 upwards	6% - 7%

The qualitative responses[32] also reveal that some respondents were not aware of the numbers of disabled students studying at their place of work.

"I am not sure of actual percentage college wide, as we only support a small minority of [those who have] *disclosed."* (FE Respondent)

"Not sure – not my area." (HE Respondent)

"We do not calculate support in this way." (HE Respondent)

"I am not privy to this information." (HE Respondent)

"5%--hard to tell though, given many different ways in which you can study here." (HE Respondent)

"Not sure – please see HESA / HEFCE figures as I am short of time." (HE Respondent)

"I am not aware of these figures being collated." (FE Respondent)

As one might expect, the proportion of disabled students varies between each organisation at which an individual works.

---

[31] We believe this is a specialist college for disabled students.

[32] There were 15 qualitative responses in total to this question (20), which can be found in Appendix 3 pages 71-72.

3.3.16 Supporting disabled students

The responses suggest that the majority of the respondents are supporting upwards of 30 students per week. It is also noted that 20 respondents reported that they are supporting 15-20 students per week.

Table 18: Disabled students supported per week

Number of students seen on a weekly basis	Frequency
0-5	8
5-10	10
10-15	6
15-20	20
20-25	4
25-30	7
30+	36

The qualitative responses[33] provide more of an insight into the numbers of students the respondents are expected to see each week and how this works in practice.

"Depends on need, there is no upper limit." (FE Respondent)

"I usually have around 44 learners at the start of the academic year knowing that some will drop out or elect not to take up the support. I usually end up with a few less than this but currently I still have 44 – some dropped out but there are more waiting in the wings to be allocated support. The FE support is divided up between Technical and Vocational support by curriculum area tutors and half an hour a week with me – that's how I can fit so many in. I have to see learners in lunch time and tea time slots so my timetable means long days with occasional gaps to grab lunch and drinks. Academic tutors are required to have 24 hours a week timetabled contact time with learners – 875 hours over the academic year." (FE Respondent)

"This includes anything from emails and telephone support to appointments." (FE Respondent)

"Too many students because we are not enough disability specialists." (HE Respondent)

"I personally see 4 students per week for needs assessments, but could be offering ongoing support to previously assessed students." (HE Respondent)

"No fixed number – demand system. Caseload was tried but proved impracticable. Around 15-20 including at least one full diagnostic assessment." (HE Respondent)

---

[33] There were 49 qualitative responses in total to this question (21), which can be found in Appendix 3 pages 72-75.

"Yearly caseload 220+ so depends on what crops up each week." (HE Respondent)

Depending on the organisation, the responses suggest there are a variety of arrangements: some have an agreed caseload and some seem to have no upper limit on the number of students they would be expected to see on a weekly basis.

Some of the variation could be explained by the different roles the respondents are undertaking, whether that is acting as an Adviser, Manager, Assessor or Tutor. To further understand the work of the respondents it would be necessary to explore this in more detail with further work.

3.3.15 Other work

To obtain a detailed insight into the work of practitioners, the respondents where asked to confirm whether or not they were undertaking additional work specific to their role. A number of the qualitative responses[34] showed that the individuals were undertaking additional work in relation to their main role. The additional work has been organised under two headings, which are 'Disability' and 'Non-disability activities'.

Examples of disability-specific activities range from undertaking DSA assessments, providing assistive technology training, 1:1 support or management of specific activities.

"DSA Needs Assessments on behalf of a QAG approved access centre."
(HE Respondent)

"Some assistive technology training." (Text Help, Inspiration, etc)
(HE Respondent)

"Not currently but I did support an OU learner in the summer break last year as the local DA did not offer support during summer. I might offer this again if she requires it."
(FE Respondent)

"Management of Deaf and Dyslexia studies." (FE Respondent)

"DSA assessor; BSL/English interpreter; support for disabled staff."
(HE Respondent)

The wide range of non-disability specific activities included acting on committees, management of student support services, working on health and safety issues, diversity and equality issues as well as providing pastoral support.

"I additionally do H&S work, advise staff, manage and appraise staff. Sit on interviews, contribute to policies and procedures." (FE Respondent)

"Liaison with Connexions, Social Services etc. Training across College, assessment of needs, management duties to include staff observation and line management, advisory

---

[34] There were 53 qualitative responses in total to this question (22), which can be found in Appendix 3 on pages 75-78.

role to director of student services and other managers / colleagues within the College."
(FE Respondent)

"Yes, Deputy Head of Student Support Services, Committee Work, Induction programme and other projects as requested." (HE Respondent)

"Non Resident House Tutor (pastoral support role for students in University owned accommodation); Display Screen Equipment Assessor; First Aider; Fire Warden."
(HE Respondent)

"Also work on Equality and Diversity issues with the E& D manager. Also coordinate Student Support (now acting up for over 2 years!)."
(HE Respondent)

Whilst a large number of respondents reported that they were undertaking additional work, it is important to note that some respondents also seemed to wonder how they would find the time:

"Absolutely not. So far, so busy." (HE Respondent)

A number of respondents have reported that they are undertaking a number of additional roles whilst undertaking their main role. These activities actually cover a wide range and could be viewed as specific roles, whether that is acting as a manager of services, assessing student need or 1:1 work with students.

3.3.16 Line Management

The responses to this question suggest there are 5 categories of staff for whom the respondents held line management responsibility:

- Disability Officers
- Dyslexia Tutors
- Support Workers e.g. note-takers
- Administrative and Clerical staff
- Other (e.g. signers, specialist ASD support and Assessors)[35]

The broad spread of categories suggests the respondents hold a broad management responsibility whether that is being responsible for specialist or administrative staff.

This question[36] also asked the respondents to identify the number of staff for whom they are responsible. 68 respondents provided further information about the types and numbers of staff for whom they are responsible. A review of the responses shows that the

---

[35] Other job titles provided by the respondents were: VL tutors, Classroom Assistants, Specialist Tutors (inc Dyslexia), Assessors, part-time tutors, First Aiders and Trainers. Not all respondents who completed this question provided job titles. Some of the responses were numerical responses.

[36] Appendix 4 provides a breakdown (category and number) of the staff each respondent has line management responsibility for. This information can be found on pages 81-86.

categories and numbers varies considerably between respondents, with staff working within a FE setting typically being responsible for larger teams.

Table 19: Line management responsibility by staff category

Category of staff	Frequency of respondents with line management responsibility
Managers	5
Disability/Dyslexia/Mental Health/Assessment Centre Managers	5
Disability Officers	21
Dyslexia Tutors	20
Dyslexia Assessors	11
DSA Assessors	7
Other Assessors	4
Support Workers e.g. Note-Takers	44
Educational Psychologists	10
Mental Health Support Workers	12
IT trainers	8
Freelancers	11
External contracted services	12
Administrative/Clerical staff	44
Other (please specify)	25

3.3.17 Day-to-day work

The aim of this question was to establish what activities the respondents undertook within their job on a day-to-day basis. 27 areas of activity were identified as being core to the role of a disability practitioner (see Table 24).

The qualitative responses[37] to this question help provide more insight into the day-to-day work of staff working to support disabled students in post-16 education.

"Day-to-day-duties: mental health promotion and awareness raising collaborating with other services to provide a network of support to students with mental health issues." (HE Respondent)

"Mainly I advise on what accessibility software is available, test trial versions of the software and advise what it can do and what I think my be useful for us to purchase. Also I demonstrate the software we have to the users and trouble shoot any technical problems they have with it." (HE Respondent)

"Additional support has grown over the last 5 years. 89% of our learners rate our services as excellent and consequently disabled learners pass their experiences of college onto other disabled people which then helps to increase our numbers." (FE Respondent)

---

[37] There were 17 qualitative responses in total to this question (24) which can be found in Appendix 3 on pages 78-79.

"I am College rep for the Disability Strand of Aimhigher." (FE Respondent)

The activities, which have been listed in Table 24, and the qualitative responses suggest that the core activities of a disability practitioner are wide ranging. The work could involve providing advice on disability legislation, working with organisational staff such as academic or administrative staff, supporting disabled students to access appropriate sources of funding and working with outside bodies as appropriate.

Table 24: Activities of a disability practitioner

	Activity	Frequency
1	Keeping up-to-date with changes within disability legislation	101
2	Supporting and advising a range of disabled students	94
2	Providing advice to academic staff on how to develop inclusive teaching and assessment practices to support disabled students	94
4	Enabling disabled students to access support for appropriate funding	83
6	Providing advice to administrative staff on how to support disabled students	82
5	Providing staff development sessions	81
7	Working in partnership with outside organisations e.g. Local Education Authorities, Social Services, Research Councils etc.	80
8	Keeping up-to-date with assistive technology/software	79
8	Raising awareness of institutional Disability Services	79
10	Providing advice to admissions staff	74
11	Acting as the lead contact within your institution on disability issues	65
11	Take part in widening participation / disability work	65
13	Providing support to disabled students studying off-campus	61
14	Managing administrative / clerical staff	51
15	Working in partnerships with local HEIs	50
16	Managing a Disability Service	48
16	Providing support to specialist staff supporting disabled students undertaking HE programmes within FE	48
18	Working in partnership with local Colleges	47
19	Reporting to an institutional Diversity and Equality Committee	44
20	Undertaking widening participation work	43
21	Managing a budget	42
20	Purchasing IT equipment, assistive technology and software	42
23	Working with Placement providers (clinical / non-clinical employers)	35
24	Reporting to an institutional Disability Committee	33
25	Providing support to disabled members of staff	28
26	Community / disability work	19
27	Managing a DSA Assessment Service	14

3.3.20 Other questions suggested by respondents

To complete the survey the respondents were asked to identify whether or not any additional questions should have been asked in the survey.

8 respondents suggested a number of questions:

"Who invented the 40 hour day that we need to do the job?" (HE Respondent)

"How well supported / resourced / respected my post is? Not!"
(HE Respondent)

"Where you see the post going and impact of 4th December 2006?"
(HE Respondent)

"What additional training would I like to see available for Disability Officers? What are the 2 most important barriers for the profession?" (HE Respondent)

"I do like my job and feel privileged to work with such a wide range of learners from Lev 2 to HE and post grads on teacher training. I find the admin required tiring and admin for 44 learners is huge so it tends to be untidy and rushed." (FE Respondent)

"Something on professional development? Like – what form does it take and what opportunities are there for?" (FE Respondent)

"Range of disabilities you support in this job? / Is support 1:1 or in class or with one student all the time etc." (FE Respondent)

These responses suggest a number of additional questions are being asked. These are about additional training, membership of NADP, impact of the Disability Equality Duty and professional development.

Any future surveys by NADP should address these questions.   Data could also be collected through NADP's one day events, annual conferences or other appropriate events.

4. Conclusions

The findings of this survey help provide a snapshot of disability practitioners and the work they are undertaking to support disabled students within post-16 education.

These results show that the majority of the respondents are already members of NADP. The majority of member-respondents have held their membership of NADP for 3 years.

When looking at the practitioners themselves, the results suggest this is a majority female profession. It is also evident that a small number of disabled people are working within the sector and have disclosed to their employer. There is an indication by some of the respondents who have disclosed their disability that they may not be receiving appropriate support.

The results of this survey help to provide an insight into the day-to-day work of a practitioner. The results suggest that the terms *Manager, Coordinator, Adviser, Assessor* and *Tutor* are titles used to describe the work of staff within the sector. The location of posts is mainly within a Student Services setting.

Most respondents are employed on a full-time basis, but this may be on either an academic or an administrative contract. The modal[38] average salary for a practitioner is within the range £25,000 - £35,000. Funding for posts seems to come from a range of internal and external streams.

In delivering support to students the majority of respondents have been working within the sector either 3-6 years or 6-9 years. The length of time in current post suggests respondents stay in their current role between 2 and 5 years.

In terms of qualifications most institutions appear to treat a bachelor's degree as the essential requirement, though a number of post-holders actually hold postgraduate or specialist qualifications. Some institutions require respondents to have a range of specialist qualities, knowledge or skills, yet others had no such requirements. Respondents argued that they brought a range of experience to the role, whether that was of already working with disabled students in post-16 education or undertaking legislative work and their comments suggested they believed this experience was important.

In the day-to-day work of a disability practitioner 27 areas of activity were identified. The priority activities ranged from keeping up-to-date with disability legislation, supporting students, working with institutional staff or helping students to access relevant sources of funding.

Other areas of activity included being responsible for managing services or budgets, working with placement providers or undertaking outreach work.

---

[38] Modal = most frequently occurring.

These responses suggest disability practitioners undertake a wide range of work within and outside the institution for which they work when supporting disabled students within post-16 education.

Appendix 1: E-mail lists contacted about the NADP survey

The following JISCmail lists were contacted to raise awareness of the survey:

- NADP JISCmail lists
- ADSHE JISCmail lists
- Dis-Forum JISCmail lists
- Dyslexia JISCmail lists
- SW DSA & WP network JISCmail lists
- Admin-Equal Opportunities JISCmail lists

Appendix 2: NADP Questionnaire

National Association of Disability Practitioners (NADP) Disability Practitioner Questionnaire

1. Are you a current NADP member?

Yes / No

2. How long have you been a NADO/P member?

☐ under 1 year
☐ 1 years
☐ 2 years
☐ 3 years
☐ 4 years
☐ 5 years
☐ 6 years
 Other (please specify ....)

3. What category of membership do you hold?

☐ Institutional
☐ Additional institutional
☐ Full
☐ Associate
☐ Student
☐ Retired
☐ International
☐ Affiliate

Additional comments
....

4. Gender: ....

5. Do you consider yourself to have a disability?

Yes / No

Additional comments
....

6. Have you disclosed your disability to your employer, and is appropriate support being provided?

Yes / No

Additional comments

....

7. What is your job title?

....

8. What is your employment status?

☐ Full-time contract
☐ Part-time contract
☐ Self-employed
☐ Hourly paid
☐ Other (Please specify: ....)

Additional comments

....

9. Who do you work for?

....

10. Is it:
☐ an FE College
☐ a Specialist College
☐ a University
☐ a Public Assessment Centre
☐ a Private Assessment Centre
☐ IT supplier
☐ other (Please specify:
....)

Additional comments

....

11. For how long have you been providing support to disabled students studying within post-16 education?
☐ 0-3 years
☐ 3-6 years
☐ 6-9 years
☐ 9-12
☐ other

Additional comments

....

12. For how many years have you being working in your current post?
- ☐ 0-2
- ☐ 2-5 years
- ☐ 5-8 years
- ☐ 8-11 years
- ☐ 11-14
- ☐ other

Additional comments

....

13. Where is your post located within the institution/company you work for?
- ☐ Student Services
- ☐ Registry
- ☐ Academic Services
- ☐ Other (Please specify:...)

Additional comments

....

14. What qualifications were required for you to undertake your current job?
- ☐ Degree
- ☐ Postgraduate qualification
- ☐ Management qualification
- ☐ Specialist qualification
- ☐ other (Please specify: ....)

Additional comments

....

15. What experience did you bring to your current post? (Briefly describe below)

16. Did the post you are currently undertaking require any specialist qualities, knowledge or skills? (Briefly describe below)

[ ]

17. What type of contract and grade are you employed on?
☐ Academic and related (Grade ....)
☐ Administrative/Support (Grade ....)
☐ Local variation to the national single pay spine (Grade ....)
☐ National single pay spine (Grade ....)
☐ Self-employed
☐ Permanent
☐ Temporary
☐ Fractional
☐ Term-Time Only
☐ Other (Please specify:..)

Additional comments

....

18. What is your current FT salary?

☐ under £15,000
☐ between £15,000-£25,000
☐ £25,000-£35,000
☐ £35,000-£45,000
☐ £45,000 - upwards

Additional comments

....

19. How is the role you undertake funded at the institution/company your work for?
☐ Disability premium funding
☐ Institutional funds
☐ Disabled Students' Allowance funding
☐ Access to Learning funding
☐ Learning and Skills Council funding
☐ A combination of the above
☐ Don't Know
☐ Other (please specify ....)

Additional comments

....

20. How many declared disabled students are studying at your place of work, and what percentage is this of the total student body?

☐ 0-100
☐ 100-500
☐ 500-1000
☐ 1000-1500
☐ 1500-2000
☐ 2000-2500
☐ 2500 upwards

Additional comments

....

21. How many disabled students are you expected to support (e.g. as a Disability Officers, Specialist Tutor, Assessor, Trainer etc ..) on a weekly basis?

☐ 0-5
☐ 5-10
☐ 10-15
☐ 15-20
☐ 20-25
☐ 25-30
☐ 30-upwards

Additional comments

....

22. Do you undertake any other work in addition to the specific disability role you are currently undertaking? If yes, please describe below:

....

23. Within your current post are you responsible for managing any staff? If yes, please circle accordingly, and state the number of staff you are responsible for.

Category of staff	No. of staff
Disability/Dyslexia/Mental Health/Assessment Centre Managers	
Disability Officers	
DSA Assessors	
Dyslexia Tutors	
Dyslexia Assessors	
Other Assessors	
Support Workers e.g. note-takers/mentors/support assistants	
Educational Psychologists	
Mental Health Support Workers	
IT trainers	
Freelancers	
External contracted services	
Administrative/Clerical staff	
Other (please specify)	

24. What do you do within your job on a day-to day basis? (Please circle one of the 3 responses)

		Your day-to-day role	Response		
			YES	NO	N/A
1.		Supporting and advising a range of disabled students			
2.		Providing advice to academic staff on how to develop inclusive teaching and assessment practices to support disabled students			
3.		Providing advice to administrative staff on how to support disabled students			
4.		Providing advice to admissions staff			
5.		Managing a Disability Service			
6.		Managing a DSA Assessment Service			
7.		Providing staff development sessions			
8.		Keeping up-to-date with changes within disability legislation			
9.		Acting as the lead contact within your institution on disability issues			
10.		Working in partnership with outside organisations e.g. Local Authorities, Social Services, Research Councils etc.			
11.		Enabling disabled students to access support for appropriate funding			
12.		Providing support to disabled members of staff			
13.		Managing a budget			
14.		Undertaking widening participation work			
15.		Keeping up-to-date with assistive technology/software			
16.		Purchasing IT equipment, assistive technology and software			
17.		Working in partnerships with local HEIs			
18.		Working in partnership with local Colleges			
19.		Working with Placement providers (clinical/non-clinical employers)			
20.		Raising awareness of institutional Disability Services			
21.		Reporting to an institutional Disability Committee			

		YES	NO	N/A
22.	Reporting to an institutional Diversity and Equality Committee			
23.	Providing support to disabled students studying off-campus			
24.	Providing support to specialist staff supporting disabled students undertaking HE programmes within FE			
25.	Take part in widening participation/disability work			
26.	Community/disability work			
27.	Managing administrative/clerical staff			
28.	Other (Please specify)			

Additional comments

....

25. Are there any other questions you would have like to have been asked?

Appendix 3: Qualitative responses to the survey questions

Question 3: What category of membership do you hold?

Responses from practitioners based in further education

- I have been involved for just one year, but the college has been involved for at least 5 years

Responses from practitioners based in higher education

- Founder member of the organisation
- Since its beginning except for a short break

Question 5: Do you consider yourself to have a disability?

Responses from practitioners based in further education

- Dyslexia
- Registered blind

Responses from practitioners based in higher education

- Partially sighted
- I would usually answer No to this question and add a note to say I consider myself to be a disabled person
- Deaf
- Mild dyslexia

Question 6: Have you disclosed your disability to your employer, and is appropriate support being provided?

Responses from practitioners based in further education

- Access to work
- I have some RSI and have received support for this
- Access to work funded equipment

Responses from practitioners based in higher education

- It is extremely difficult to be positive about my employer's attitude towards staff with disabilities. I will not even go into what they do to students. It is all lip-service. No, no substance!
- Had to make own arrangements for support

- Not enough consultation regarding the impact of actions such as closing car parks or doing refurbishments to office building ie. Lack of impact assessments
- Although disclosed in 2004 little has been done to support me in spite of an Access to Work assessment and recommendations being sent to HR
- Yes, I have disclosed but no, I do not think appropriate support is being provided
- Some support has been provided

Question 7: What is your job title?

Access Ability Team Leader
Access Centre Manager/Academic Support Tutor
Additional Learning Needs Adviser
Additional Learning Support Manager
Additional Support Co-ordinator
Additional Support Guidance Adviser
Additional Support Manager
Assistant Registrar, Equality and Diversity
Centre Manager, Centre for Inclusive Learning
Client Services Manager
Deputy Head of Student Support Services / Disability Adviser
Director
Directory Student and Learning Support
Disability Adviser x12
Disability and Learning Support Officer
Disability Co-ordinator x7
Disability Manager
Disability Officer x7
Disability Services Manager (x3)
Disability Support Adviser
Disability Support Co-ordinator
Disability Support Manager
Disability Support Officer
Disabled Students Officer
DSA Assessor (x3)
Dyslexia Co-ordinator Senior Lecturer
Dyslexia Co-ordinator x2
Dyslexia Diagnosis and Support Co-ordinator
Dyslexia Support Tutor x2
Dyslexia Tutor
Dyslexia Tutor Assessor
Dyslexia/Disability Consultant
Equality and Diversity Officer
Facilitator
Head of Disabilities Service
Head of Disability & Dyslexia Service
Head of Disability Service
Head of Disability Support Unit
Head of Student Support

Head, AccessAbility Centre
IT Officer
Learner Support Tutor
Learning Support Coordinator
Learning Support Tutor – Dyslexia
Mental Health Adviser
Programme Manager for Additional Support
Programme Manager: Learning Support
Project Manager and Research Fellow
Section Leader
Senior Adviser (Disability)
Senior Development Officer
Senior Disabilities Adviser
Senior Disability Advisor x 3
Senior Disability Officer
Senior Dyslexia Tutor
Senior Educational Support Officer
Senior Special Needs Trainer
Specific Learning Difficulties Advisor
SpLD support tutor
Staff Disability Advisor
Student Adviser (Disabilities)
Student Adviser/Team Leader for students with a Physical Disability
and Medical condition
Student Services Manager
Student Support Manager
Student Welfare Officer
Study Skills Support Tutor
Study Skills Tutor
Subject Leader GIS
Teacher
Team Leader – Disability Team
Team Leader Additional Support
Widening Participation Coordinator (remit for disabled students)
Widening Participation Officer

Question 8: What is your employment status?

Responses from practitioners based in higher education

- I am employed directly by the university on a contract basis of 400 hours per year and also take on extra DSA referrals which are LEA funded

---

Question 10 Is it: FE College/a Specialist College/University/Public Assessment Centre Private Assessment Centre/IT supplier/Other?

Responses from practitioners based in further education

- This is a small (250 students) specialist contemporary dance college with a Foundation Course, Bachelor of Performing Arts course and Graduate courses
- It's an NNAC/QAG-listed centre in an FE College

Responses from practitioners based in other institutions/organisations

- I also do 2 days per week on a temporary hourly paid contact at XXX University as an XXX Adviser
- 6th form college
- Adult Community Learning
- Charity

Question 11: How long have you been providing support to disabled students studying within post-16 education?

Responses from practitioners based in further education

- I have been providing support for students with disabilities for 19 years. The centre I now work for has been providing formal support for approx 11 years
- In FE college - 16 years. In YTS (1980s) 5 years. Within the Careers Service. (1970 / 1980s) 12 years
- 25 years +
- Came into post in 2001
- For approx 15 years

Responses from practitioners based in higher education

- Since 1988
- I am saddened to see that greedy Universities push more and more work to their disability staff while de-skilling them to titles such as 'advisors'?
- More than 12 years
- Overlapped until 2 years ago with also being a part time FE lecturer
- I provide support for disabled students in the School of Science and Environment and advise colleagues on disability issues. I liaise with the Disability Officer on behalf of students and staff in our school
- 20 years in an FE college, full time. 4 years in present post, 0.4.
- (Prior to all of that, many years' teaching in special schools)
- Myself currently 13 years but the university for 15 years as having a named adviser
- The university has been providing support for disabled students for over 13 years; my job share partner and I have been in post for 18 months
- I have taught in post 16 for 24 years of which 10 has been as an assessor and support tutor and undertaking staff development. Prior to that my work as a tutor has an inclusive education profile

- Since 1993
- 20 years in support
- My current role involves supporting disabled staff, but sometimes this includes people who are both a member of staff and a student (eg. Graduate Teaching Assistant / PhD student)
- Over 20 years
- 14 years including previous HEFCE-funded project in XXX University
- Over 12 years

Responses from practitioners based in other organisations/institutions

- 25 years or so!

Question 12: How long have you being working in your current post?

Responses from practitioners based in further education

- In the early part of my time here I also taught groups of adults with learning disabilities at Entry and Level 1 - Life Skills, Lit, Num, Independent living skills

Responses from practitioners based in higher education

- My post is academic and the disability part is additional to my academic duties. It was not considered in the recent pay framework job evaluation

Responses from practitioners based in other organisations/institutions

- 18 years

Question 13: Where is your post located within the institution/company you work for?

Responses from practitioners based in further education

- For some bizarre reason we were located within one academic school, and taken away from Student Support
- The post is being looked at and may be located elsewhere
- Additional Learning Support
- Skills for Life
- Under review
- Business Support
- Learner Services

Responses from practitioners based in higher education

- Reshuffle after reshuffle you get sick of it
- Equality Service
- Student Services is part of Registry
- We should be part of learning services and advice
- Welfare Services. Encompasses Disability Support, Counselling, the Chaplaincy & Finance Support
- Equality Unit
- Disability Resource Centre
- Locating the service in academia is vital to ensure change to practice is more effective – role includes exam boards and validations etc
- Student and Academic Services
- Student Services sits within the Academic Registry
- Library Services – I assist the Library Accessibility Officers on technical/IT matters such as the operation of assistive technologies
- Skills for Life
- Library Services
- Library Information Services
- Equality and Diversity department
- Occupational Health. Occupational Health is part of the Human Resources Directorate
- I am not convinced that Student Services is the correct place for support for disabled students
- Skills for Life – Study Support
- Research Lab

Question 14: What qualifications were required for you to undertake your current job?

Responses from practitioners based in further education

- Experience, but also had a nursing background. The job has been evolving rapidly and my previous experience has been invaluable to help me to manage staff and develop this role. There has been little on training for disability across the college for teaching staff, so I have had to find my way independently
- Cert Ed
- Degree & specialist qualification & experience
- While no specific formal qualifications were required for the post it did ask that candidates have knowledge and experience of working with students with disabilities
- Degree also required
- Degrees, PCGE
- I have a degree (BSc Hons – Education and Technology OU). I also had a Dyslexia qualification and agreed to also obtain the OCR Cert in SpLD
- Including a specific qualification in disability
- Good standard education IT skills; experience
- PG Cert SPld, degree, PGCE

- There were no qualification requirements. Previous experience, aptitude and being a friend of someone already doing the job were the key factors
- Also teaching cert

Responses from practitioners based in higher education

- Relevant experience
- Management qualification
- I specialise in D/deaf students so needed interpreting & BSL qualifications Other Disability Coordinators here do not need specialist qualifications
- Experience. I trained as a Needs Assessor at XXX, after completing a BSc (Hons) in Business Information Systems at XXX University
- Plus a line management qualification
- Understanding of dyslexia initially required and teaching experience. Like most of my colleagues I also have a post graduate qualification – though not in this discipline
- Both degree and management qualification
- Level 4 qualification
- Appropriate experience
- Am undertaking a doctorate – Accommodated assessment for experience students in Art and Design AMBDA was required for the role together with Masters level qualification in another area
- HE level of qualification HNC Care Practice
- Life/work experience would have been taken into account
- As I began as the only XXX and XXX Officer at XXX College XXX and then developed Disability Support at XXX, I wrote a lot of my job description and the three that preceded it. This involved a lot more than just having a degree
- A degree and a professional/postgraduate qualification were desirable criteria for the post. I have both.
- Knowledge and experience of sector required
- Postgraduate degree
- Dyslexia qualification
- Degree, PGCE, specialist dyslexia qualification (AMBDA)
- I have teaching cert and SpLD cert

Responses from practitioners based in other organisations/institutions

- Not quite sure, as I was taken on by both employers based on experience and an MEd in Special Educational Needs (HE & PSAC Respondent)
- PG. Specialist Qualification. Currently undertaking a management course

Question 15: What experience did you bring to your current post?

Responses from practitioners based in further education

- Nursing background in NHS. Also private sector and social services with learning disabled people
- I had 10 years' experience working with students with dyslexia and study skills problems
- Years if working in LLDD considerable experience with students with disabilities and management qualifications
- Multi tasking; knowledge of referral process; DSA advice; teaching and learning support; counselling; management of a team of Inclusive Learning Tutors
- Experience in supporting long-term unemployed disabled adults to re-train and gain skills for employment. Job coaching support for disabled adults. Disability training and support for businesses and organisations
- Time as Learning Support Assistant, work with adults with autistic spectrum disorder, time teaching basic skills
- Worked as the Assistant MIS Manager for 3 years in the college. I was trained as a Foster Carer by Social Services. I have 10 years Customer Service experience
- Specialist Teacher –SEN/Experience working with LEA/Tutor for LDD/D/ Understanding of Funding Mechanisms/Understanding of HE Finance including DSA
- Support roles within compulsory education sector –special school, mainstream and emotional / psychological /behavioural unit
- I managed a training programme for students with disabilities for 12 years and had been working in that area for 19 years. I was involved in a number of Government funded projects to establish inclusive practices for students with disabilities pre-SENDO and I also was involved in a project that helped established the Centre for Inclusive Learning, that I now manage full time
- Many years of teaching in First and special schools and teaching and supporting adults in FE mainstream and specialist provision
- SENCO, Head teacher and experience of working with OfSTED in schools
- Experience of working with dyslexic learners in employment who could work well on the job but struggled to obtain relevant qualifications through day release to college
- Highly experienced first aider, many years experience working with disabled young people and child protection issues
- Built on close to 30yrs experience working with students with additional support needs of all kinds
- I worked in Social Services at a centre for disabled people before coming into post. I had a good knowledge of legislation and the benefits system for disabled people.
- Worked in support at 2 other colleges as a support tutor. Had experience of assessing and supporting learners
- 8-9 years as a support worker in the college and supporting the co-ordinator
- Working with 14-19 year olds and adult learners. Teaching N.V.Q. BTEC nationals and F.D. Level work in the vocational area of Beauty Therapy
- Disability knowledge from a range of educational and care settings. EBD, Learning Difficulties in residential care with education. Over 16 years of FE experience supporting learners with difficulties/disabilities and other barriers across all areas of curriculum. Management of a team of support staff

- Dyslexia Assessment, diagnosis, support, Irlen Screener, I run a PG Cert in Adult Dyslexia Diagnosis and Support
- An understanding of assessment of need and the HE context. Personal experience of disability and impairment through nursing & degree qualifications, various university posts including teaching & research at undergraduate and postgraduate level
- Years teaching in Special Ed; all age groups and disabilities

Responses from practitioners based in higher education

- Working in University for a long time but no experience in disability save for experience as parent of disabled child
- Experience: Previous role involved co-ordinating exam/academic support for students with additional needs, otherwise I didn't have any direct disability-related experience
- 4 year experience teaching children with Asperger's. 2 Years experience teaching adults with learning difficulties. Musical experience necessary to support musicians
- Extensive experience of working in the public sector including the Civil Service and the NHS. Also worked for a large customer service department for a major industrial company
- Experience of working with disabled students for over 15 years. Experience of assessing for DSA – previous ACCESS Centre Manager
- I was a Graduate Trainee within the Registry and therefore had a fairly good knowledge and experience of how the College worked. I also had a lot of contacts within XXX. Finally, my research and teaching experience have also helped me comprehend the different models of disability and fulfilling the training requirements of the job
- Working with students since 1988, providing ALL student services. Specialised in "disability" support since 1991
- High level management skills and deep understanding of disability skills directly related to higher education. Being disabled I can work from a personal perspective and not simply a theory based. I am an individual and I bring a unique perspective to my role
- I worked in FE as a lecturer to students with learning difficulties and/or physical disabilities, Mental health Co-ordinator and finally ALS Manager, managing 50 support staff and a budget of £1,025,000
- 20 Years of working with students with disabilities, experience of working in DHSS benefits office and civil service
- Worked in the University for 16 years with varying student contact. I learnt my skills on the job and took extra courses as required. Progressed from administering Student Support Worker provision to Disability Adviser. Successful application to Senior Adviser (Disability) role
- 2 years support work with people with disabilities - residential/community. 1 year support work with people with learning difficulties - employment
- Substantial experience in D/deaf education, all sectors inc HE, BSL/English interpreter, MA in Deaf Studies, knowledge of DSA Assessments, as a trainer inc of staff to work with D/deaf & disabled students
- Three years f/t needs assessing, with experience in Visual Impairment, Hearing Impairment, and Mobility Issues
- Background of supporting students in higher education; teaching deaf adults for ten years; DSA assessments for ten years; involved in and managed various HEFCE

projects. Carried out the first Survey of Disability Officers in HE in 2001. Glad to see it is now being updated
- Degree, campaigning and casework experience
- Previous teaching experience in post-16 education, previous technical support for disabled students, previous disability adviser experience
- Over 20 years experience in CRE as policy officer, then senior policy officer. 2 years experience of equality and diversity work in another university
- Very little experience of supporting disabled students. But experience of higher education
- Have specialist qualification and wide experience in Mental Health. In addition I have a teaching qualification
- 7 years experience as a Specialist Careers Adviser for disabled children and young people
- 10 years as a trainer in central govt, several years as a researcher in social policy working for national charities and housing associations, 5 years in FE
- Teaching and research experience
- Working within student services at a different university - providing NMPA support for disabled students. Line Management experience. Academic understanding/Ph.D. (previously also taught at a university)
- Twelve years working in disability information and advice services (voluntary sector). Project management. General management
- Worked with individuals with a range of disabilities in a training and coaching capacity. Involved in the development of an accreditation framework within the Further Education sector which included the development and approval of credit based qualifications for specific target groups
- I have a PGCE as well as my diploma in special educational needs. I have worked as a teacher in SEN and mainstream schools as well as, as a dyslexia tutor
- Experience in interpreting the DDA and providing support to colleagues as well as influencing senior stakeholders. No previous experience in the education sector
- Modern languages degree, Diploma of Teacher of the Deaf, special school teaching, 20 years managing support for deaf students at FE level (and some HE) – then same for students with other disabilities
- Working in the disability field for approx 8 years prior to moving into HE sector
- Disability Adviser and Project officer at another University. Prior to that was a note taker, support worker, key skills tutor in HE and FE
- Very little direct disability experience, 10 years experience of working with and supporting students. Plus managerial and budgeting experience
- I had worked in the department and had a little experience. Training has been provided to bridge any gaps
- Over 8 year's experience of working in an advisory role to disabled students in HE. Several years' experience of working as an assessor. Supervisory experience. Experience of delivering staff development sessions, creating university policy
- Previously managed a project for adults with disabilities to gain qualifications in IT, journalism, business admin etc
- Worked within organisations of disabled people; worked in field of equality and diversity
- 5 years CAB advice (Voluntary and paid). 2+ years general welfare advice in another HEI. 4 years setting up and running a Student Union Advice Centre
- Personal experience of family members dyslexia. Experience as subject tutor at university level. Cert SpLd

- Development Officer SL Open College. PGCE FE Greenwich Teaching Methodology. Prep for HE tutor Study Skills Course director Humanities Access. Tutor on BA & MA programmes Sheffield Hallam. A level Examiner – Sociology. Researcher into non standard entrants at University of East London. 10 years GCSE/A level Access tutor. 2 years Counselling. 1 year YTS and C & G teaching
- I have worked with students who have a learning difficulty and/or disability and/ or medical condition for at least 15 years. I provide training in the SENDA legislation to staff and work as a consultant in this area for LSDA – training for staff in colleges
- Similar position in other University
- Previous experience as a teacher trainer and as a tutor
- Teacher
- Dyslexia specialist working with adults in education and the workplace
- Qualified teacher – post 16 ed. Taught at specialist residential college. Co-ordinated outreach learning support service in FE. DSA assessor. Braille and assistive tech skills. At current institution, worked as Development officer (carried out institution wide audit in relation to policy and procedures) and produced Code of Practice for QA Handbook. Also worked as Disability Adviser and Co-ordinated Support Workers Scheme
- High level of disability related and advice work experience in a number of sectors. Knowledge/experience of DDA
- Experienced with using a range of software, and providing data in a range of electronic formats. Am a ex Nurse so also experienced working with people with varied needs
- Teacher of the deaf status and level 2 BSL
- Worked as Special Exam Arrangements co-ordinator (hourly paid) on a casual basis for a number of years
- Linguist (MPhil)/25 year of EFL tutor/Academic Skills tutor University experience
- Over ten years working with people with disabilities. A wide range of disability related qualifications. Many of those years working in post 16 education
- 1 year working as an administrator in a Disability Office of another Uni, Other admin experience and HE admissions experience
- Experience with working with students with physical and learning disabilities. Experience supporting students in Higher Education
- Previous role included supporting students with additional needs, particularly in relation to making exam arrangements/reasonable adjustments
- Range of employment in various aspects of disability
- Teaching at post 16; PGCE; LLLU Adult Dyslexia; managed programme in adult education (Islington)
- 1) Teaching (English); 2) Administration   a)Dean of Students at an International HEI; b) Welfare & advice work; c) main point of contact for students & staff with disabilities 1990-1996 (only welfare officer/disability officer)
- Qualified social worker. Worked in statutory and voluntary sector in disability services prior to HE
- 13 years experience of supporting disabled people in various settings (housing and social care, employment and training and learning support)
- 20 years experience of working with disabled learners and over 10 years of management experience
- Fifteen years mainstream/SEN teaching in primary schools
- University Lecturing/Study Needs Assessor

- Project management / Supporting and managing staff/ Writing project proposals/ Staff development/ Disability equality & consultation/ Range of provision for disabled students in HE/ Networking & liaison/ICT
- Screening and tutoring dyslexic students
- As a qualified teacher in FE – subject areas, core skills, adult literacy & learning support, I had extensive experience of conducting needs assessments and working with students with a wide range of needs
- 35 years as a professional working with disabled people and wide ranging knowledge of Assistive Technology
- MSc SpLD, experience in primary sector
- 25 yrs of teaching, experiencing mild dyslexia and living with a severely dyslexic daughter
- Wide experience of working with students with special educational needs in all areas of education: primary school, secondary school, FE and HE. NVQ and Dyslexia assessments
- PhD; Widening Participation Student Ambassador; Experience of working with schools
- Telephone help line experience/technical computer experience /research skills (quantitative and qualitative)/ interviewing skills
- Previous work in higher education institution and also background in Disability funding (at HEFCE)

Responses from practitioners based in other organisations/institutions

- Background in co-ordinating the educational programme for learners with severe learning disability (ACL respondent)
- Specialist teacher in State, Independent education and private Adult tuition

---

Question 16: Did the post you are currently undertaking require any specialist qualities, knowledge or skills?

Responses from practitioners based in further education

- No, but it has hugely benefited from my experience
- People skills. Being an advocate.
- Years if working in LLDD considerable experience with students with disabilities and management qualifications
- Dyslexia Qualifications; PGCE; Management qualification
- Team management experience/Knowledge and experiencing of working with disabled people. Knowledge of DDA and DED. Presentation, communication skills etc.
- Management. Budgets. Legislation etc.
- Relevant experience
- The post required knowledge of current legislation in relation to disability, SENDO, DDA etc. It also required me to understand the funding systems for supporting students with disability across a range of FE & HE provision. I needed to display management skills in terms of a budget, staffing etc. I also needed to be involved directly with students and various organisations external to the college, parents, carers etc. The job

also required a knowledge and background in training for staff on disability and equality issues

- Experience supporting students, teaching qualifications
- Full Teaching qualification, specialist Post Grad. (I hold a Post Grad cert. in Aspergers), management experience and training
- No requirement - only management experience although have knowledge and experience of disability & teaching those with learning difficulty helped with strategic and operational decisions
- Not essentially but I am sure that one reason I was successful was down to the fact I had worked with 14 - 19 age group for many years and I had elected to study modules linked to special education for my OU degree which I obtained in the second year of my job here
- There was a requirement to have a knowledge of the difficulties which post-16 students with disabilities would face in a large environment. Also there was a requirement to have a good understanding of how to provide support in a wide variety of learning environments
- No, but knowledge of where to get support like this is essential
- First Aid, Counselling Skills, DDL, H & S
- RSA in Counselling; Diploma in social sciences; Certificate in deaf blind awareness in Sign languages
- Not particularly but good organisational and people skills help
- Disability and management mainly. Funding, data analysis, legislation etc.
- This part time post is Equal Opportunities Adviser for the college as well as responsibility for disabled students (physical sensory impairment). Another member of staff coordinates all learning support and is effectively in charge of specialist learner support services
- Yes- diagnosis and support
- Knowledge and experience in Specific Learning Difficulties

Responses from practitioners based in higher education

- On-the-job training was provided to bring me up to speed with policies, procedures, legislation etc and I attended a number of training sessions and conferences in my first year to broaden my knowledge
- Braille, Music Reading, Music Computer skills, Disability Awareness Training experience, Assistive software
- In depth knowledge of disability, assessing, knowledge of current legislation
- Knowledge of DDA legislation, knowledge of different disability, management skills, diplomacy, remaining clam under pressure
- Disability and other relevant legislation need to be a good advocate and negotiator; flexible and able to respond "on the hoof" to situations
- Management skills; Understanding of specific learning difficulties; Interpersonal skills; Problem solving; managing staff of approximately fifty people; managing complex budgets; managing expectations of students
- Knowledge about disability and disabling environments/ Knowledge about benefits/ Institutional knowledge (admissions, student records, examinations processes)
- Training to be an assessor. Specialist courses in order to advise and insist sight impaired and hearing impaired students.

- General Interpreting, communication with D/deaf people, experience in HE experience and understanding of HE.
- Three years f/t needs assessing, with experience in Visual Impairment, Hearing Postgraduate qualifications. Management experience/ qualifications/ research skills. Impairment, and Mobility Issues
- Knowledge of disability issues (ideally in HE environment)
- DA experience and knowledge of legislation, DSA process, HE, etc.
- Knowledge of equalities legislation; awareness of the key issues around equality and diversity in HE sector, including disabilities
- Have specialist qualification and wide experience in Mental Health. In addition I have a teaching qualification.
- Experience of working with disabled students, understanding of Higher Education, knowledge of Disability legislation, Management of staff and budgets
- Good interpersonal skills
- Awareness of academic teaching and learning requirements at undergraduate and postgraduate level, teaching experience, expertise in the nuts and bolts of literacy
- Knowledge and skills appropriate to lecturing in a specialist subject in HE. Management skills re. curriculum development and administration
- I.A.G. skills and generic assessment skills. I possess assessor and internal verifier awards.
- Knowledge of UK legislation and disability issues in an educational environment line management and budgetary skills
- Understanding the HE sector as well as the processes to support disabled students. Learning about the DSA and Needs assessment processes. Understanding more about dyslexia and how this impacts learning
- Knowledge of and experience with deaf/hard of hearing learners, and blind/partially sighted learners, and all issues related to their learning needs. Knowledge of assessments, HE environment & procedures, relevant local & national networks & agencies
- Understanding of disability issues and legislation. Experience of delivering presentations.
- DSA knowledge, BSL Level One, knowledge of DDA, experience of working with disabled people, experience of HE environment
- Knowledge of disability legislation and how it relates to HE. Knowledge of funding available to disabled students/Knowledge of the impact of different disabilities on student's learning experience. Knowledge of teaching and learning process.
- Knowledge and understanding of disabilities, how disabilities impact on studies, ability to identify and organise support for individuals.
- Knowledge of disability legislation and social model of disability; personal experience of being a disabled person; ability to negotiate with academic staff, senior management and LEAs etc
- Study skills 24 years at all levels. The experiential re. dyslexic father, brother and son. Understanding of Cultural Studies (MA related for decoding briefs and suggesting alternative texts, audio etc. Curriculum Development. Staff Development. PGDip Prof Studs Ed dyslexia from D.I. Pastoral care experience counselling experience. Up date training is CPD
- Specific Learning Difficulties knowledge
- Disability Awareness/Dyslexia qualification/Academic experience/ Communication skills
- Not really - transferable skills I had from teaching, but found I had to learn a lot fast!

- A dyslexia postgraduate qualification and some experience of working in HE
- Experience of working in HE sector. Desirable to have worked within the field of learning support/disability service. Knowledge of disability issues and legislation.
- Understanding of impact of disability on access to /involvement in studies. Understanding
- Already possessed most of the knowledge and skills needed but I needed to learn in greater detail the operation of our accessibility software/systems of impact of DDA. Advice skills. Quality assurance.
- Plenty! Experience and understanding, disability awareness and beyond, customer service skills, networking/liaison skills, and a bit of campaigning spirit!
- A Certificate in SpLD
- Disability legislation, knowledge of disability related support, DSA
- Good Customer Service and admin skills, knowledge of Disability legislation, experience of working in a HEI, ideally with disabled students
- Good Communication skills, able to manage workload. Experience with many different type of disability and support
- Experience of supporting disabled people, managing teachers
- Experience and knowledge of HE, disability, disability legislation, etc.
- Disability; Counselling skills; Disability legislation; Management; Budgetary control
- Knowledge of DDA, assessment skills, skills in supporting people with different needs, knowledge of different impairments assistive technology, ergonomics, health and safety
- Knowledge of support for disabled learners and of current legislation
- OCR Diploma for teachers of learners with SpLD
- Understanding of HE, disability issues, assistive technologies
- Project management / Supporting and managing staff/ Writing project proposals/ Staff development/ Disability equality & consultation/ Range of provision for disabled students in HE/ Networking & liaison/ICT.
- adaptive technology/creating accessible documents/developing disability equality policies & procedures/ QA issues (for matrix accreditation)/ Disability legislation & DED/ basic employment legislation
- No - it's possible to teach self the job on the job
- Dyslexia qualification
- Extensive knowledge and experience of working with students with SpLd's; experienced needs assessor; strong people skills
- Knowledge of disabilities, assistive technologies, e-learning, web accessibility and research skills
- Ability to carry out full and screening assessments as well as offer tutorials
- Yes a qualification in Dyslexia
- Specialist Dyslexia qualification
- Knowledge of UK school system; project management; experience of applying for funding
- Knowledge of assistive technology including apple macs knowledge of recent legal matters such as DDA and pd and FOI
- Verbal and written communication skills/listening interviewing skills, including the ability to respond with sensitivity and empathy to students in distress/Analytical thinking & creative problem-solving skills/ability to develop & deliver training courses Knowledge of assistive technology and ICT skills/ An understanding of general disability issues as they affect higher education/An understanding of a wide range of specific physical and

mental impairments and the ability to translate this into practical support strategies for students in higher education.

Responses from practitioners based in other organisations/institutions

- Past experience and knowledge clearly helped. Required to know the legal responsibilities under the various acts (ACL respondent)
- Specialist dyslexia PG Dip (VS Respondent)
- I think both roles require an in-depth knowledge of the support requirements of students with learning difference, physical and hidden disabilities. An understanding of the human condition helps and also having knowledge of how to set boundaries and a sense of empathy aids the process of organising appropriate support. Utilising open questions and active listening is vital and knowledge of the institution's systems is important!

Question 17: What type of contract and grade are you employed on?

Responses from practitioners based in further education

- I manage a team of 22 but this is not particularly reflected in my pay
- Grade due to be re-classified on single spine but no info yet

Responses from practitioners based in higher education

- Moving to single pay spine soon, hopefully getting pay rise, work load increased 10 fold
- We have just been restructured to level out variations between the 2 campuses - my grade is now 7
- Just moved onto new pay scale so cannot give current grade. Now called professional and support
- Currently undergoing HERA
- To be reviewed under HERA
- It was part time at first but with 29% of learners claiming a disability it is been full time for the last 4 and half years
- I had an academic contract as a dyslexia tutor in another HEI, but Local contract in the current HEI
- Specialist Welfare Band 7
- An AR grade would be much more appropriate as the majority of my tasks are not administrative.

Responses from practitioners based in other organisations/institutions

- Permanent hourly paid contract with XXX and Temporary hourly paid contract with XXX

Question 18: What is your current full-time salary?

Responses from practitioners based in further education

- Under review

Responses from practitioners based in higher education

- With London Weighting. In the £15,000 – 25,000 bracket without the London weighting
- We are underpaid and undervalued
- 0.5 post so pro rata
- My grade encompasses some managerial responsibilities. Other tutors are on grade 5
- It is less than an equivalent post at most of the other universities
- At the bottom end of this scale. I think HERA has made a wider gap between pay of colleagues in high level support roles (such as disability adviser) in different universities. Everything is more variable now not standardised at all as was promised

---

Question 19: How is the role you undertake funded at the institution/company your work for?

Responses from practitioners based in further education
- Disabled Students Allowance and Work Based Learning Funding
- DSA; LSC ALS funding; Work Based Training funding
- DEL (NI)
- FE Additional Support claim

Responses from practitioners based in higher education

- Combination of WP and institutional funding
- Disability premium funding and a bit of DSA
- Some of our funding can come from multiple funding
- HEFCE
- All activities in the centre are income generating – no direct funding. So mainly via the DSA
- Started with a role as Teaching and Learning and then undertook qualification – not sure of funding streams
- Post is mostly core funded but percentage is funded by premium funding as well
- I have taken this role in addition to my other work roles. (IT Training, support, production of documentation etc)
- It may be a combination of the first two
- We do have a part-time member of staff that is funded through DPF
- Services are funded by DSA,ALF and institutional funds
- I also do extra work that is funded via Disabled Students' Allowance funding

Responses from practitioners based in other organisations/institutions

- Project funding – complicated as it is embedded into different projects funded by LSC, ESF, Lottery, grants etc

---

Question 20: How many declared disabled students are studying at your place of work, and what percentage is this of the total student body?

Responses from practitioners based in further education

- I am not sure of actual percentage college wide, as we only support a small minority of disclosed
- Student numbers – total 10,303 of which 928 have declared disabilities. (interestingly – staff numbers 714 of which 7 have declared disabilities)
- 29% last year claiming to have a disability. 24.5% total up to the present day
- I am not aware of these figures being collated

Responses from practitioners based in higher education

- 17% approx on this campus – do not have the figures for the Hull campus
- In my school there are around 7% disabled students. I believe this is about the same for the institution
- We do not calculate support in this way
- 400 are registered with DSA at LCC but the University has similar numbers at the six other colleges
- 600 in 19,000 students
- 5%--hard to tell though, given many different ways in which you can study here
- 100-500 disabled staff which represents 3% of the total. [figure of 100-500 included above]
- 1000-1500 – 6% = Dyslexic/SpLD only

Question 21: How many disabled students are you expected to support (e.g. as a Disability Officers, Specialist Tutor, Assessor, Trainer etc ..) on a weekly basis?

Responses from practitioners based in further education

- Depends on need, there is no upper limit
- I co-ordinate support
- I also have considerable management responsibilities
- This includes anything from emails and telephone support to appointments
- I have a specialised team of 20-30 doing the work, I manage the service
- Varies term on term
- I usually have around 44 learners at the start of the academic year knowing that some will drop out or elect not to take up the support. I usually end up with a few less than this but currently I still have 44 – some dropped out but there are more waiting in the

wings to be allocated support. The FE support is divided up between Technical and Vocational support by curriculum area tutors and half and hour a week with me – that's how I can fit so many in. I have to see learners in lunch time and tea time slots so my time table means long days with occasional gaps to grab lunch and drinks. Academic tutors are required to have 24 hours a week time tabled contact time with learners – 875hours over the academic year

- Figures vary current diploma of 80 learners 18 claiming a disability. Our pathways there could be from 0 to 30 every week. Take in to account residential aspects of our short courses
- As the Co-ordinator for Disability Support (which does not include SpLD) I do not support any – but my dept supports approx 110 per week. The SpLD team support approx 120 students per week
- Varies as core of the task is transition arrangements. Students then supported by others
- 23 hours contact time

Responses from practitioners based in higher education

- Yearly caseload 220+ so depends on what crops up each week
- 112 student out of 550ish 20% of student body
- Too many students because not enough disability specialists
- We also have a duty adviser system so see a high number of students on a weekly basis in addition to our caseload where contact may vary
- I organise the Note taking Scheme (25 students), plus drop-in/guidance/ enquiries/ DSA Assessments… plus interpret for 1 or 2 per week
- I personally see 4 students per week for needs assessments, but could be offering ongoing support to previously assessed students
- Not stated in any contract. As many as declare themselves which makes it difficult to manage caseloads
- None directly as manage the service overall
- I do not have a disability caseload of any size
- Students are supported by the whole Disabilities Service Team – we do not have a caseload model. The team includes Head of Disabilities Service, Mental Health Adviser, Disabilities Adviser (Dyslexia), Disabilities Adviser (Sensory Support), 2 x Dyslexia Tutors, Technical Adviser, Support Worker Service Coordinator 7 approx 40 support workers
- Have responsibility for 150 students with range of SpLD but better to look at hours per week of support – should average out at 20 – 24 a week (my .5 post with 8 sessional hours from a colleague) plus a .5 admin worker. Not all students take up one to one support but we are not meeting the increasing demand for support at the moment
- 25-30: This is the maximum that I could be expected to support but in reality I see only a few of them
- I work with approximately 60 students, most of whom don't require regular contact once they are settled into university life
- No formal targets agreed- support provided as necessary
- No student contact at present – strategic development only
- Varies and numbers are not expected. We have days allocated where we see students and depending on the query depends on the length of time allocated. Some can be 15 mins others can be 1 hour

- The figure is for both job share partners and split over three campus sites
- These students are now specialist they are undertaking accommodated assessment and is a max number. I am PATOSS registered and assess or deliver staff development or research
- I allow for around 3 x 1 hour appointments per day. On two days I allow an additional 2 hours so a total of 20 hours. Various tasks associated include dyslexia screening, DSA advice, referral for study support, liaison with other staff on adjustments...Concerned with assessing students and referring and advising appropriately
- Varies according to time of year
- No defined number – very much on an as needs basis, in addition to seeing new students, and monitoring and review of known students. Also see prospective students
- Other staff within the team also have responsibilities to support learners and support staff are employed to support specific students
- I support any who present but numbers are confidential so in my role I am not privy to the information
- This is both available appointments, drop in sessions and other contact (ie phone or email)
- The support varies but we currently have over 150 'active' clients who have regular support requirements, review meetings etc
- See 5-10 disabled staff per week. Average number of staff supported on a weekly basis
- My main function is NOT direct student support: I work on policies and procedures
- Typically 5-10 in 0.5fte post, but considerable variation with time of year –may see up to 10 per day during busiest periods such as exam applications
- All 1:1 support
- Research work involving at least 30 students
- I have seen 53 dyslexic students this year.
- No fixed number – demand system. Caseload was tried but proved impracticable. Around 15-20 including at least one full diagnostic assessment

Responses from practitioners based in other organisations/institutions

- I have a team of staff who give part of their time to disability support – teachers and learning support assistants

---

Question 22: Do you undertake any other work in addition to the specific disability role you are currently undertaking?

Responses from practitioners based in further education

- I additionally do H&S work, advise staff, manage and appraise staff. Sit on interviews, contribute to policies and procedures
- Teaching on the University of Plymouth PGCE/CeRT. Ed. On Inclusion and Widening Participation
- It is a very wide reaching role – management and lots of aspects of the disability 'umbrella.'

- Lead on DES. Training staff on disability issues. Advise on accessible marketing, premises, activities etc
- Also work on Equality and Diversity issues with the E& D manager. Also coordinate Student Support (now acting up for over 2 years!)
- Enrichment/Disability and Equality Committee
- Child protection officer. Course tutor (all special programmes courses, including Transition for pre school leavers)
- I provide information sessions to statutory and non statutory organisations. I am involved in advice and guidance for prospective students. The centre also provides DSA assessments for external candidates as we are the only recognised access centre in N Ireland
- Liaison with Connexions, Social services etc. training across College, assessment of needs, Management duties to include Staff observation and line management, Advisory role to director of Student services and other managers/colleagues within the College
- I have ALS, Key Skills, Nursery, Creche, Foundation Programmes, Skills for Life discrete programmes, Embedded learning of Entry to Level 2 programmes, Discrete programmes for SLDD and ALDD, Student Services (Registry, Admissions, Careers, IAG, Enrolment etc)
- Not currently but I did support and OU learner in the summer break last year as the local DA do not offer support during summer. I might offer this again if she requires it
- Manager of all learning support activities, ESOL and Skills for Life provision across the college
- In charge of first aid throughout the campus, including teaching FAW etc. Child protection issues
- Management of all Student Support functions, eg tutorials, student finance, counselling, IAG, ALS plus teaching
- I'm on a number of committees.
- I have responsibility for all E&D issues concerning learners
- Nothing different to my job description, which includes: recruitment staff training advising on new build projects etc
- I am not in a disabilities teaching role but I do have a disabled learner in my tutor group
- Management of Deaf and Dyslexia Studies
- Major part of role is Equal Opps Officer e.g. policies schemes etc.
- Separately as an Associate Lecturer (taking an evening class)

Responses from practitioners based in higher education

- DSA Needs Assessments on behalf of a QAG approved access centre
- Access Centre Manager and Academic Support Tutor
- Also expected to manage the service, provide staff development, contribute to policy, strategic planning, attend various committees etc. etc.
- Absolutely not. So far so busy
- Yes, Deputy Head of Student Support Services, Committee Work, Induction programme and other projects as requested.
- Harassment Adviser
- DSA assessor; BSL/English interpreter; support for disabled staff
- Some assistive technology training (texthelp, Inspiration, etc)

- DSA Assessor
- Strategic and policy work
- As manager of an E&D unit that covers the provision of disability support services for students, I have to cover the broad range of issues relating to both service provision and policy development work linked to E&D
- I undertake assessments of students' study related needs to inform recommendations for DSA. I provide advice and guidance to colleagues at all levels in our institution on reasonable adjustments and compliance with the DDA and Equality legislation.
- Training, health promotion, liaison with external and internal individuals and organisations
- Member of Student Services Senior Management Team. University lead on disability issues
- Outreach Widening Participation work
- Staff awareness, occasional lectures to education students on SpLD
- Assistant Manager and Assessor
- Also involved in Assessment of Needs; advising on access, policy and disability issues; consultation with other departments
- DSA assessor, although this is becoming less frequent and needs to be reviewed
- Deputise as manager of the department
- Yes. Supporting Accessibility is a relatively small part of my overall role
- Study Skills support
- Some managerial responsibilities/Advisory role/Staff development training/Study Skills teaching on summer school
- Disability awareness training
- DES action plan review & update; Staff training; Policy writing; Strategic planning
- Non Resident House Tutor (pastoral support role for students in University owned accommodation); Display Screen Equipment Assessor; First Aider; Fire Warden
- Manager of Assessment Centre
- Management of dyslexia tutor team, invoicing of tutoring to LA's
- Also work with adults with learning disabilities and carry out assessments at other times
- Help with workshops for dyslexic students
- Dyslexia support tutor to students that are DSA funded

Question 24: What do you do within your job on a day-to-day basis?

Responses from practitioners based in further education

- Additional support has grown over the last 5 years. 89% of our learners rate our services as excellent and consequently disabled learners pass their experiences of college onto other disabled people which then helps to increase our numbers
- School Liaison; Manage ALS
- I am College rep for the Disability Strand of Aimhigher.

Responses from practitioners based in higher education

- We are underpaid for what we do. I would earn more if I were to work in a private sector. I do not think they have looked into how the sector has changed and, unfairly kept the salary low
- Day-to-day-duties: mental health promotion and awareness raising collaborating with other services to provide a network of support to students with mental health issues
- Policy Development
- Our institution is not very proactive and our manager and director of student support services control our training allowance, block our requests for training and development, do not encourage research and development work and try to suppress any positive work we do. They are the most useless and ineffective pair and I am embarrassed and shocked at their attitude and further shocked that they are in their positions
- I only hope my colleague who is Disability Support Officer here responds- since she does the admissions work, institutional DDA responsibility and manages the support workers
- Drafting policies; overseeing DES Action Plan progress; recruiting/managing NMPAs
- Policy development; SpLD screening
- Recruit, train and supervise support workers. Match support workers to students
- Research and fellowships for handbooks and feedback; examinations and moderation; project management staff are not permanent but eg Into Art with Dyslexia £78K budget was my project 2 years ago. Now onto small budget for handbooks external liaison design work etc.
- Mainly I advise on what accessibility software is available, test trial versions of the software and advise what it can do and what I think my be useful for us to purchase. Also I demonstrate the software we have to the users and trouble shoot any technical problems they have with it
- Research
- Assessment; screening; academic skills tutorials
- Screening and tutoring dyslexic students

Question 25: Are there any other questions you would have like to have been asked?

Responses from practitioners based in further education

- I do like my job and feel privileged to work with such a wide range of learners from Lev 2 to HE and post grads on teacher training. I find the admin required tiring and admin for 44 learners is huge so it tends to be untidy and rushed
- Range of disabilities you support in this job? / Is support 1:1 or in class or with one student all the time etc.

Responses from practitioners based in higher education

- Who invented the 40 hour day that we need to do the job
- How well supported / resourced / respected my post is? Not!

- How has role analysis affected your job? it has affected more than just pay/salary
- Where you see the post going and impact of 4th December
- Would you like to be a member of NADP?
- What additional training would I like to see available for DOs? What are the 2 most important barriers for the profession?
- Something on professional development? Like – what form does it take and what opportunities are there for?

Appendix 4: Breakdown of staff by category and number

Responses to the following question:

'Within your current post are you responsible for managing any staff? Please state the category and number of staff you are responsible for.'

Category of staff		Staff Numbers
HE Respondent		
Dyslexia Tutors x2	Support Workers x40	44
Educational Psychologists x1	Administrative staff x1	
HE Respondent		
Dyslexia Tutors x5	Support Workers x2	8
Administrative staff x1		
HE Respondent		
Disability Officers x1	DSA Assessors x1	19
Dyslexia Tutors x1	Dyslexia Assessors x3	
Support Workers x4	EP x3	
Freelancers x5	Administrative staff x1	
HE Respondent		
DSA Assessors x4		4
HE Respondent		
Dyslexia Tutor x1	Support Workers x50	57
External x2	Administrative staff x2	
Study for WPx1	Other x1	
FE Respondent		
Support Workers x16	Mental Health Support Workers x4	22
Student Adviser for VI	students x1	
Other x1		
HE Respondent		
Disability Officer x1	Dyslexia Tutors x6	34
Support Workers x20	Mental Health Support Workers x1	
Staff IT Trainers x1	External staff x4	
Administrative staff x1		
HE Respondent		
DSA Assessors x1	Dyslexia Tutors x17	50
Dyslexia Assessors x1	Support Workers x7	
EP x9	Freelancers x6	
External x5	Administrative x4	
HE Respondent		
Support Workers x40		40
HE Respondent		
Disability Officer x1	Support Workers x40	41

Category of staff		Staff Numbers
HE Respondent		
Support Workers x30	Freelancers x5	35
FE Respondent		
Staff Managers x1	Mental Health Support Workers x8	12
IT Trainers x1	Administrative staff x2	
HE Respondent		
Administrative staff x1		1
FE Respondent		
Dyslexia Tutors x12	Support Workers x12	101
Mental Health Support Workers x2	Administrative staff x2	
Classroom assistants x23	CSW x10	
Number x10	Other x30	
HE Respondent		
Disability Officers x3	Dyslexia Tutors x3	39
Support Workers x30	Administrative staff x3	
HE Respondent		
Support Workers x12	Administrative staff x1	13
HE Respondent		
Disability Officers x6	Dyslexia Tutors x4	18
Dyslexia Assessors x2	EP x2	
IT Trainers x1	Administrative staff x3	
HE Respondent		
Disability Officers x5	Administrative staff x2	9
Other (Mentoring Support Worker) x1	Other x1	
HE Respondent		
Disability Officers x1	Support Workers x5	7
Administrative staff x1		
HE Respondent		
Disability Officers x3	Dyslexia Tutors x2	40
Support Workers x35		
HE Respondent		
Staff Managers x1	Disability Officers x2	49
Dyslexia Tutors x2	Support Workers x40	
Administrative staff x2	Technical Adviser x1	
Other x1		
FE Respondent		
Dyslexia Tutors x1	Dyslexia Assessors x1	45
Support Workers x30	Mental Health Support Workers x1	
External x2	Administrative x2	
Literacy and Numeracy Tutors x1	Other x7	

Category of staff		Staff Numbers
HE Respondent		
Dyslexia Tutors x10	Educational Psychologists x3	16
Other x3		
HE Respondent		
Dyslexia Tutors x1 (8 hrs per week)	Administrative staff x1 (0.5)	2
HE Respondent		
Lecturing Colleagues x1	Other x3	4
FE Respondent		
Support Workers x12	BSL interpreters x1	15
Other x2		
HE Respondent		
Staff Managers x1	Dyslexia Tutors x 5	59
Mental Health Support Workers x1	IT Trainers x1	
Freelancers x48	External x1	
Administrative staff x2		
HE Respondent		
Freelancers x15	External x2	18
Administrative staff x1		
HE Respondent		
Disability Officers x2	Dyslexia Tutors x3	32
Support Workers x24	IT trainers x1	
External x2		
FE Respondent		
Staff Managers x3		3
HE Respondent		
Disability Officers x3	Administrative staff x2	5
FE Respondent		
Disability Officers x1	Support Workers x27	39 +
Educational Psychologists on demand	External staff – RNIB on demand	
Specialist tutors 11 (inc dyslexia)		
HE Respondent		
Support Workers x30	Freelancers x2	34
Administrative staff x2		
FE Respondent		
Freelancers varies	Trainer	1
other x1		
FE Respondent		
Staff Managers x2	Disability Officers x2	45
DSA Assessors x5	Dyslexia Tutors x2	
Dyslexia Assessors x2	Support Workers x30	
Administrative staff x2		

Category of staff		Staff Numbers
FE Respondent		
Dyslexia Tutors (3 permanent 10 plus part-time)	Assessors part-time tutors x20	25
Support tutors with teaching and assessing duties x2		
HE Respondent		
Support Workers x50		50
HE Respondent		
Disability Officers x2	DSA Assessors x2	16
Dyslexia Tutors x6	Dyslexia Assessors x1	
Educational Psychologists x1	Freelancers x2	
Administrative staff x2		
FE Respondent		
Dyslexia Tutors x1	Dyslexia Assessors x1	172
Support Workers x164	External x1	
Administrative staff x2	Signers x1	
Other x2		
FE Respondent		
Dyslexia Tutors x12	Support Workers x5	18
Administrative staff x1		
HE Respondent		
Assessors x1	External x1	3
Other x1 relative to projects		
FE Respondent		
Staff Managers x1	Dyslexia tutors x1	14
Support Workers x10	Administrative staff x1	
Classroom Assistants x1		
HE Respondent		
Dyslexia Tutors x2	Support Workers x15	22
External x1	Administrative staff x4	
FE Respondent		
Staff Managers x5	Support Workers x7	15
External x2	Administrative staff x1	
HE Respondent		
Dyslexia Tutors x5	Educational Psychologists x4	15
Administrative staff x5	IT Trainers x 1	
FE Respondent		
First Aiders x1	Other x45	46

Category of staff		Staff Numbers
FE Respondent		
Staff Managers x1	Dyslexia Tutors x1	27
Support Workers x21	Mental Health Support Workers x1	
Administrative staff x3		
HE Respondent		
Dyslexia support adviser x1	Other x1	2
FE Respondent		
Dyslexia Tutors x3	Dyslexia Assessors x1	35
Support Workers x26	Mental Health Support Workers x4	
Administrative staff x1		
FE Respondent		
Support Workers x 10		10
FE Respondent		
Support Workers x 30	Administrative staff x1	31
HE Respondent		
Disability Officers x2	Support Workers x45	49
Administrative staff x1	Other x1.	
HE Respondent		
Disability Officers x2	Mental Health Support Workers x1	3
He Respondent		
Dyslexia Tutors x5		5
FE Respondent		
Support Workers x54		54
HE Respondent		
Support Workers x12		12
HE Respondent		
Disability Officer x1	Dyslexia Tutor x5	7
Administrative staff x1		
HE Respondent		
Disability Officer x1	Dyslexia Tutor x1	38
Support Workers x35	Educational Psychologist x1	
HE Respondent		
Disability Officers x2	Mental Health Support Workers x1	3
HE Respondent		
Disability Officers x2	Dyslexia Tutors x3	21
Support Workers x10	Freelancers x5	
Administrative staff x1		
Respondent		
Dyslexia Tutors x 18	Support Workers x35	66
Administrative staff x2	Communication Support Workers x1	

Category of staff		Staff Numbers
Other x1	Teacher of Deaf and Deaf Services Manager x2	
Other x2	VL Tutors x3	
Other x2.		
FE Respondent		
Dyslexia Tutors x2	Assessors x4	41
Support Workers x30	Freelancers x3	
Administrative staff x2		
HE Respondent		
Dyslexia Tutors x1	Support Workers x40	44
Mental Health Support Workers x1	Other x1	
Specialist ASD support		
FE Respondent		
Dyslexia Tutors x3	Dyslexia Assessors x3	9
Educational Psychologists x3		
HE Respondent		
Dyslexia Tutors x 10	Support Workers x10	22
Administrative staff x2		
VS Respondent		
Dyslexia Tutors x3	Dyslexia Assessors x5	18
Freelancers x5	Administrative staff x3	
HE Respondent		
Dyslexia Tutors x6		6
HE Respondent		
Dyslexia Tutorsx2	Support Workers x 2	5
Administrative x 1		

Appendix 5: Acknowledgements

I would like to take the opportunity to thank the disability practitioners who completed this survey as well as the support of the NADP Board in completing this briefing.